Hauntings

GAIL B. STEWART

THE LIBRARY OF
Ghosts & Hauntings

ReferencePoint Press®

San Diego, CA

Picture credits:
Cover: IStockphoto.com
Maury Aaseng: 7
AP Images: 17, 35, 41, 44, 46, 51, 53, 58, 69
Dreamstime: 55
IStockphoto.com: 15, 26
Landov: 11, 12
North Wind: 31

Series design and book layout:
Amy Stirnkorb

LIBRARY OF CONGRESS CATALOGING-IN-PUBLICATION DATA

Stewart, Gail B. (Gail Barbara), 1949-
 Hauntings / by Gail B. Stewart.
     p. cm. -- (The library of ghosts and hauntings)
 Includes bibliographical references and index.
 ISBN-13: 978-1-60152-092-0 (hardback)
 ISBN-10: 1-60152-092-1 (hardback)
 1. Ghosts. I. Title.
 BF1461.S856 2009
 133.1--dc22

                                                                         2009001537

Contents

Introduction

"I Guess No One Wanted to Live Here"

Did You Know?
Every nation on Earth has ghost or spirit haunting stories.

It was in 2006 that Martha (who does not wish to have her last name used) and her family moved into their Chicago home. She says they had saved money for the down payment on a house for years and were excited when they found what seemed to be the perfect one on the city's South Side. It was close to everything—schools, a park, and the bus line. She and her husband could be at work in less than a half hour.

"It was great." Martha pauses. "At least for a little while. Until we discovered that it was haunted."[1]

"The Footsteps Were Very Light, Like a Child's"

She says that strange things began happening within a week of moving in. First of all were the odd noises, especially at night. She and her husband Tony slept in the downstairs bedroom, while their three children had rooms upstairs. "The first time we heard the footsteps was on a Sunday night," Martha remembers. "The kids were in bed, and I was in bed reading. Tony was taking the dog on a short walk. And I started hearing footsteps right above

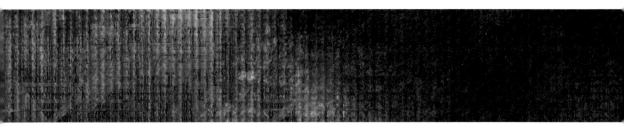

me, in what was our daughter Angie's room. The footsteps were very light, like a child's."[2]

Martha assumed Angie had just gotten up to use the bathroom, but the noises kept on for several minutes. "I went upstairs but the lights were all off," she says.

> Angie was sleeping, there was no activity at all. When Tony came in from walking the dog, he heard it, too. He did the same as I did—went up and looked around. But nothing. We were both spooked, but by the next morning we kind of shrugged it off. Maybe it was just that the house was old—wooden floors creaking or maybe a mouse. Anyway, in the light of day, it didn't seem spooky at all.[3]

Increasing Spookiness

But over the next few weeks, new developments made them even more uneasy. The footsteps had become an almost everyday occurrence. Sometimes it seemed as though someone were running or skipping, other times just walking. But always they were in Angie's room. "She never heard anything, but we did—all the time," says Martha. "During the day, late at night."[4]

In addition, Martha noticed strange cold spots in the living room. "This was really bizarre," she says. "I'd sit down in the green chair next to the piano and it would

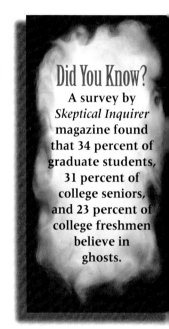

Did You Know?
A survey by *Skeptical Inquirer* magazine found that 34 percent of graduate students, 31 percent of college seniors, and 23 percent of college freshmen believe in ghosts.

be ice cold. I'd stand up and walk three feet away and the temperature would be warm again. There was no way to explain this. No drafts, no open window, nothing. And the difference in temperature was at least 30 degrees, so it was really obvious."[5]

"No Hollywood Ending"
Frustrated and a little nervous, Martha and Tony finally decided to contact a psychic. Many people who hire a psychic start out by insisting that they themselves do not believe in ghosts. "But I admit, I do believe," Martha says. "I was open to it. So was Tony, but maybe not as much as me. But if you'd heard those footsteps upstairs, and felt those icy spots in the living room, you maybe would have believed anything was possible."[6]

The result, however, was not what she and Tony had hoped. Though the psychic said she could sense the presence of a little girl's spirit, she was not able to convince the child to leave. "Ellen [the psychic] did a couple of ceremonial things, burning incense and saying prayers," Martha says. "And at first it seemed to help. The noises and the cold spots went away for maybe a couple of days. But then everything started again, and we knew we had to move. It wasn't the outcome we were looking for— no Hollywood ending, where the spirit goes to the other side and everyone is happy. But I will say the experience made me more of a believer."[7]

Ghosts and Haunting
Martha's story is more common than many people may think. In a 2005 poll conducted by CBS News, 48 percent of Americans surveyed said they believe in ghosts, while 7 percent said they are unsure. Even more surprising, 22 percent of Americans say that they themselves have seen

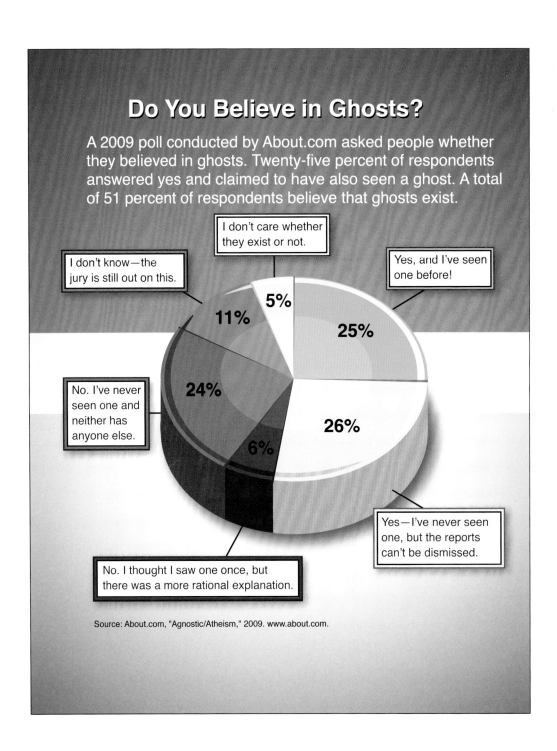

Source: About.com, "Agnostic/Atheism," 2009. www.about.com.

or felt the presence of a ghost.

A ghost is believed to be the spirit of a person who has died. Most religions of the world teach that when one dies, the spirit goes to a spirit world, such as heaven. But some spirits do not leave. They choose not to move to the spirit world but decide to remain on Earth. When they decide to stay, they are known as ghosts. And many of those ghosts haunt, or linger in, a particular place—a house, a school building, a cemetery, a ship, and so on—that had some special meaning to them when they were alive.

Ghost hauntings have been reported all over the world, dating back thousands of years. And ghosts have revealed themselves to people in hundreds of ways. As Martha and her husband learned, unexplained cold spots in rooms and footsteps are two common ways. One Minneapolis man and his children heard ghosts bouncing balls in their house. A woman in Ireland says she has a ghost who sometimes plays simple tunes on her piano in the middle of the night. A man in Ohio has seen a white mist hovering over his wife's grave and believes it is her spirit.

Sometimes ghostly activity turns out to have less-than-ghostly origins. Yet many cases of hauntings seem to have no good explanation, and researchers say these accounts should not be dismissed as nonsense. "For now, the most we can say is that there is good evidence to indicate that ghosts exist," says Elle, a Chicago ghost researcher. "And . . . they're haunting everything from old spooky houses and cemeteries to beauty parlors and office buildings. Given time, I think technology is going to prove it."[8]

CHAPTER 1

Why Ghosts Haunt

Although the afterlife is portrayed by most religions to be one of peace and happiness, a lot of spirits seem to prefer to remain on Earth. Ghost researchers say they believe that spirits refuse to leave for several reasons. According to Midwest ghost researcher Grace Donne, the lack of an appropriate funeral or burial can be an important reason that ghosts cannot rest and are unable to make the crossing from death to the afterlife.

"We tend to think of funerals as being for the living," she says, "but when we look at the reasons spirits do not cross over [into the spirit world], it may actually be just as important to the spirit of the deceased. For those spirits, the funeral ceremony is a way for them to know that their time on earth is over, that they were loved, but that they no longer reside here."[9]

Ghosts in the Water, Ghosts on the Shore

After a deadly tsunami in Thailand, Indonesia, and Sri Lanka in 2004 residents reported seeing thousands of ghosts haunting the shores and villages where people perished. The tsunami had killed almost 250,000 people, and tens of thousands more were missing and presumed dead.

The bodies of the dead were laid out in long rows, and rescue workers hoped that family members would recognize and claim the bodies. But as the weeks went by,

thousands of the dead had not been claimed, and as a result very few funerals took place. Local residents began complaining of ghosts haunting villages along the shore as well as the shallow water of the ocean. The ghostly sightings were not entirely unexpected, says Thai psychologist Wallop Piyamanotham.

"Thai people believe that when people die, a relative has to cremate them or bless them," he explains. "If this is not done, or the body is not found, people believe the person will appear over and over again to show where they are."[10]

The most upsetting occurrences were voices from the sea calling for help and the sight of ghostly mothers walking along the shore screaming for their children. In some cases, the voices of foreign tourists were reported singing and laughing at night on the beach, but when searchers investigated, they found no one there.

Helpful Haunting

But a lack of burial is only one reason for hauntings. Some ghosts appear for a more positive reason—to help people in need. One November in the 1930s, on a dangerous rocky point on Lake Superior, a young teenager saved the lives of dozens of sailors with help from her grandfather. As strange as it may seem, her grandfather had been dead for years.

The girl, now an elderly woman who has asked that her name not be used, had been raised on that lake point. Her grandfather had been the keeper of the lighthouse—and it was no easy job. In those days, as today, lighthouses were an important way to keep sailors from crashing into the shore in dark or stormy weather. But unlike today, lighthouses in those days were not automated. The wick had to be lit by hand,

The devastating 2004 tsunami left behind twisted metal, upended houses, and ruined lives in Indonesia (pictured) and elsewhere. Also left behind, according to witnesses, were the ghosts of thousands who died when the tidal wave crashed ashore.

and the oil flow had to be carefully adjusted to provide enough power for the light to burn brilliantly enough to be seen by ships miles away.

Her grandfather had died under tragic circumstances. It was during a sudden wild winter storm with icy winds and monstrous waves. Ships on Lake Superior were in danger, for they could not see the shore without the light. But the light never came on. One ship crashed into the reef, and half of the crew died. When people went to the lighthouse to find out why it was not lit, they found the old man dead on the stairs. He had apparently been running to light the lamp when he suffered a heart attack.

"I Couldn't Do It!"

Years later, another winter storm hit the lighthouse point along Lake Superior. Though the girl's father was now the lighthouse keeper, he was ill with a high fever and could not leave his bed. He told his daughter that she had to do it—and that he had confidence in her.

But though she had watched both her grandfather and father light the lamp many times, she had never done it herself. Nervously she tried to light the wick and slowly regulate the brass damper that would supply oil to the lamp. But she was failing miserably. She was trying to work quickly, but her hands were shaking. All she could think about were the sailors out in that storm who were depending on the light, and she would be to blame if it were not lit.

Just as she became convinced the job was too much for her, she told writer Frederick Stonehouse, something amazing happened:

> Suddenly, I heard Grandfather's soft voice behind me. "Slow down, girl, you can do it.

OPPOSITE: A woman in Thailand searches rows of bodies in hopes of finding a loved one who went missing after the tsunami. With thousands of dead, many bodies were never claimed and funerals were not held— leaving the spirits of victims free to seek out family members.

13

Those sailors depend on you." Despite the wind, I clearly heard him. Turning quickly, I saw my grandfather standing right behind me. . . . There was nothing misty about him, either. He was as solid as I am. His blue eyes still sparkled like always. He looked right at me and said, "I failed once, but not again. Just take your time. You watched me do it enough. You remember how."[11]

She did just as he said, and she was able to light the wick. When she turned around, her grandfather was gone. It seemed that his ghost had returned for just a short time, to make up for what he had failed to do years before.

Needing Something

In many cases, ghosts haunt a location because they are looking for something. It is, say ghost researchers, as though the spirit is unable to rest without it. Take the case of William Miller, a colonel in the Union army in the U.S. Civil War. He was killed in the battle of Gettysburg in July 1863, after which he was given the Medal of Honor.

For years after his death frightening moans and screams could be heard near his grave at Gettysburg National Cemetery. A psychic was eventually called in, and told the cemetery staff that the sounds were made by the spirit of William Miller. Evidently, the psychic explained, Miller's ghost was anguished because his tombstone did not list the Medal of Honor. Once that information was added to the grave marker, the eerie cries ended.

Another ghost that needed something in order to cross over to the spirit world was that of Molly, a young girl who died sometime in the 1930s while playing outside of

Did You Know?
A poltergeist is a type of spirit that haunts people, whereas a ghost is usually tied to a particular location.

Many lighthouses are said to be haunted. A teenage girl claimed the former keeper of one such lighthouse—her dead grandfather—helped her save the lives of a group of sailors.

her Florence, Alabama, home. As always, she was with her dog—the love of her life. This particular afternoon the dog ran into the street, and Molly lunged to save him from an oncoming car. The car could not stop, however, and Molly and the dog were killed.

Shortly after she died, neighbors were shocked to see her outside playing. When they ran outside to get a better look, she disappeared. Though it has been more than 75 years since her death, Molly's spirit continues to haunt the area. People say they still see a little blond girl on the balcony of her former home. Sometimes she talks with neighbor children, asking them to help her search for her missing dog. Many residents think she is reluctant to leave for the spirit world without her canine best friend.

A New Will

Ghosts have other reasons to linger. One is unfinished business—something very important that needs to be explained or corrected so that the spirit can finally rest. That seemed to be the motivation of the ghost of James L. Chaffin, a North Carolina farmer who died in 1921. Chaffin's will indicated that the farm and all of his money would go to his third son, Marshall.

But in 1925 his son James was woken from a sound sleep to see his father standing before him, wearing his favorite coat. The ghost did not speak but kept pointing to the inside breast pocket of the coat. Rattled, James went to his mother's house the next morning to get his father's coat, but she told him she had given it to his brother John. Taking a witness with him, James visited John the next day. The coat was found in the back of a hall closet, the inside pocket stitched shut. They opened the pocket and found a note in which their

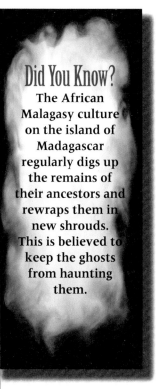

Did You Know?
The African Malagasy culture on the island of Madagascar regularly digs up the remains of their ancestors and rewraps them in new shrouds. This is believed to keep the ghosts from haunting them.

Dead soldiers lie on the Civil War battlefield at Gettysburg. The spirit of one of the dead, Colonel William Miller, was said to have moaned and screamed for years until a psychic discovered the cause: the soldier's grave marker made no mention of his Medal of Honor.

father said he had made a new will and had placed it in the family bible.

When the bible was opened, they found a will, dated 14 years after the original one. In this new will their father had left all of the property equally to the sons, as long as they looked after their mother. It was definitely their father's handwriting, and the court ruled that it was genuine. Did the ghost of James L. Chaffin really lead to the discovery of the later will? No one can say for certain, but no one has ever provided an alternate explanation either.

The Greenbrier Ghost

A similarly helpful spirit is said to have changed the course of events in Greenbrier County, West Virginia, in 1897. On January 23 of that year, Zona Heaster Shue was discovered dead in her house. Her husband, Erasmus Stribbling Trout Shue—known to townspeople as "Trout"—had sent his apprentice Andy to the house to see if Zona needed anything from the store. When the apprentice got there he found her lying dead on the floor, her body cold and her eyes open.

He ran back to tell Trout, and local doctor George Knapp was called to examine her and determine the cause of death. When he arrived, he found Trout seemingly beside himself with grief. Trout had already carried Zona's body upstairs and had laid her in their bed. He had already dressed her for burial, too. Writes ghost researcher Troy Taylor, "A high-necked, stiff-collared dress covered her neck and a veil had been placed over her face."[12]

Trout cradled his wife's head in his arms and sobbed—making it difficult for the doctor to examine her. Knapp was sympathetic to the grieving husband, however, and,

La Llorona

One of the most famous ghosts, legendary in Mexico and parts of Central America, is La Llorona, or the Weeping Walker. She fell in love with a man who did not want children. However, she already had several children, and she drowned them so that he would be with her. Afterward, she was consumed with guilt over what she had done and killed herself. She is said to haunt riverbanks or deserted roads. Thousands of people have reported seeing her walking alone at night, sobbing and crying out for her children.

as he admitted later, he gave the body only the briefest examination before determining that she had likely died from falling down the stairs after fainting.

"The Ghost Turned Her Head Completely Around"

A few weeks later, according to local stories, Zona's spirit appeared to her mother, Mary Heaster, who was suspicious about her daughter's death. The spirit, Heaster later told neighbors, first appeared to her as a bright light, then a shimmering ghostly body took form. The air in the bedroom, said Heaster later, became very cold. The ghost said that Trout had murdered her because she had not served him meat for his supper. He had been abusive before, she said, and cruel. This time, he broke her neck. "To show this [to her mother]," writes Taylor, "the ghost turned her head completely around until she was facing backwards."[13]

Heaster went to the local prosecutor and told him her story. The prosecutor agreed to reopen the case so that doctors could more carefully examine the body for evidence of a crime. On February 22, 1887, the body was exhumed, or dug up. In the presence of five jury members and assorted onlookers, doctors performed an autopsy. They saw immediately that she had not died in a fall. According to the death certificate, "the neck was broken and the windpipe mashed," and on her throat "were the marks of fingers,"[14] indicating that she had been choked.

Trout was arrested and jailed for the murder of his wife. Had it not been for the ghost of Zona Heaster Shue, the crime might never have come to light. At least that is how the story goes. Could there be other explanations for how this crime was uncovered?

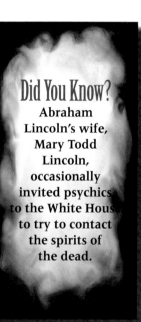

Did You Know?
Abraham Lincoln's wife, Mary Todd Lincoln, occasionally invited psychics to the White House to try to contact the spirits of the dead.

Maybe It Was Not a Ghost?

Katie Letcher Lyle, a Virginia researcher who was especially intrigued by the story, has come up with another explanation for the discovery of how Zona died. Many residents of the town knew that Heaster did not like her son-in-law. She had witnessed him being verbally abusive to her daughter and considered him a dangerous bully. Heaster's opinion of Trout—and some information about him that came to light in the weeks after her daughter's death—could have validated her suspicion that he had murdered Zona.

The information, which sent the town buzzing, was that Trout had been married twice before, prior to his coming to Greenbrier County. He had beaten his first wife so badly, Lyle writes, "that a group of vigilantes dragged him out of bed one winter night and threw him through the ice in the Greenbrier River."[15] His second wife died under mysterious circumstances only eight months after their wedding.

Lyle believes that this information made Heaster all the more certain that Trout was a murderer. Perhaps because she sensed that the townspeople were superstitious and therefore more likely to believe the story if a ghost were involved, she invented the story of the spirit. On the other hand, no proof has been found that the ghost story was an invention by Heaster. She lived almost 20 years after Trout Shue was sentenced to life in prison and never recanted her story. The story of the Greenbrier Ghost has remained a mystery, as have most other ghost stories that have survived through the years.

Did You Know?
A certain kind of haunting that lasts only a minute or so is called a "crisis apparition." This ghost appears at the moment of death to say good-bye to a loved one.

CHAPTER 2
Hauntings in the Great Outdoors

For many people the term "haunted" usually brings to mind a creaky old house. Actually, hauntings can take place anywhere—including the outdoors. It appears to make no difference whether the location is a road, a quiet cemetery, or a schoolyard. Reports of ghosts—some of them well-documented—seem to come from every location imaginable.

Nothing Unusual

One of the least likely spots to meet a ghost was found by a woman named Jenny, who for a time lived with her young son in Tucson, Arizona. Neither the location of this ghost nor the ghost itself was at all spooky. In fact, the ghost Jenny met was as unthreatening and unghostlike as one could imagine.

Jenny's little boy wanted to go fishing one day, and though she had never gone fishing before, she was determined to try. They went to a lake outside the city to fish from shore, but she soon became frustrated because she could not cast or even bait the hook very well. As she struggled with her son's fishing gear, a young man in his twenties came up behind her and offered to help. He showed them how to bait the hook so the worm did not fall off, and he showed Jenny and her son how to cast.

He was a pleasant man, and Jenny felt comfortable

enough to invite him to join them in a picnic at the lakeshore afterward. He accepted, and the three had an enjoyable time for the rest of the afternoon. She had brought her camera and taken a picture of him and her son as they posed with the fish they had caught.

The next day, after getting the film developed at a one-hour photo shop, she decided to have another copy of the picture made so she could share it with him. He had told her his name and the name of the store where he worked. But when she called the store to make sure he was in, things got strange very quickly.

An Appalling Discovery

The receptionist connected her with a supervisor who was less than friendly. Jenny repeated her request, and the man asked what her business was. A little annoyed by his attitude, she quickly explained that she simply wanted to give the man she had met a photo to repay his kindness the day before.

The supervisor then asked her to describe the man she had met, and she did. According to ghost researcher Brad Steiger, "the man gasped and said that she had described perfectly his younger brother who had drowned at that lake five years before."[16] Though she disbelieved the man at first, Jenny checked newspaper records at the library and saw that the man who had drowned was definitely the man who had been so kind the day before—although it seemed impossible to believe.

The story is strange, but the postscript is even stranger. Not knowing much about the young man she had met, Jenny wondered why his ghost was not able to cross over into the spirit world. Though she realized her behavior would seem strange, she said later that she went to the spot along the shore where they'd met and "spoke into

Did You Know?
Some researchers think cold spots are actually portals through which ghosts transport themselves.

the lake, as if she were addressing him face-to-face."[17] She told him that he would be at peace if he stopped haunting the world—specifically, the lake where he drowned—and instead crossed over into the spirit world as he was supposed to. She also told him that she would pray for him.

Late that night, a telephone call woke her from a deep sleep. The line was static-filled, as though the call was coming from a long way away. Then she heard only two words: "Thank you." The caller never identified himself, but Jenny believed it was her new friend and that he had finally realized he needed to move on.

The Haunted Farm Field

Another unusual place for an outdoor haunting is a farmer's field. But that is exactly where a widely publicized haunting took place in 1892. It happened in Fernandina, Florida, and the ghost first appeared to a man named Peterson—himself a farmer.

Peterson was sitting up with a sick child one night when he saw a strange sight out the window. A man was outside, driving a plow pulled by a team of oxen. He later explained to a reporter that the sight was odd, for not only was the man plowing Peterson's cornfield, but he was doing it at midnight.

Peterson was also struck by how vivid the scene was. "The animals, man, and plow were all as plain to be seen as if it had been daylight," the *Aberdeen (Kansas) Daily News* reported later, "though the rest of the field was in comparative gloom."[18] He also told newspaper reporters that the man "was dressed in the clothes of a laborer, and wore a large broad-brimmed hat, which completely concealed his features. He seemed intent on his work and never raised his head; when he cracked his whip . . . over

the backs of the oxen, there was no noise."[19]

Peterson called his oldest son to go outside and find out who the man was. But as his father watched from the window, the boy walked right through the man and the plow, as if they were not there at all. He returned, saying he had not seen anything at all. When Peterson himself went outside, he realized that he was unable to see the plowman either—yet when he returned to his child's sickroom, he could see him perfectly.

Baffled, the next day he told neighbors about what he had seen, and many of them came over to the house to witness what seemed to be a ghost plowing his field. They, too, saw the ghost from the window, and like Peterson, when they went outside for a closer look, they could not see him at all. Several of the neighbors believed the ghost could be that of the man who owned the land before Peterson. He was reputed to have committed suicide in that very field, although the reasons were unknown.

"I Hate That Place"

While a sunny lakeshore and a farmer's field may be surprising places to witness a ghost, certainly a cemetery is far less so. Many hauntings have been reported at cemeteries. And none has had more eerie stories attached to it than a tiny abandoned graveyard in central Illinois.

It is called Old Union Cemetery, and it used to belong to a church. However, in 1931 the church burned down, and the graveyard and the road nearby became overgrown and unused. Occasionally a county worker would come out to cut the grass and clear away rubbish, but otherwise, it was simply forgotten.

But it has not been forgotten by nearby residents. They talk about very strange occurrences within the cemetery—especially in one particular section. It is a

Fog shrouds an old graveyard in Canada. Cemeteries have long been a favorite location for stories of hauntings.

private plot, although the tombstones are no longer legible. The section is set off from the rest of the cemetery by a decorative metal fence.

In this private plot, eerie balls of colored light dart among the tombstones. And, as researcher Troy Taylor learned from interviewing witnesses, unexplained gusts of cold air seem to hit visitors to the plot. It seemed, one told Taylor, "that it was almost like someone opened the door of a giant icebox and let all the cold air out."[20]

"I hate that place," says Gary, a county worker who used to cut grass at the cemetery. He says that the private plot was always inexplicably cold and that he had an odd feeling whenever he was there. "I felt," he says, "like someone was watching me."[21]

A sheriff's deputy agrees, saying that she saw first-hand what spooked workers and residents. "I used to get reports from people who lived out that way who said that they saw lights in Old Union cemetery at night," she says. "They thought vandals were in the graveyard. I never found any vandals or anyone else out there, but I did see these lights in the back. They flew around all over the place. The place gave me the creeps."[22]

Did You Know?
Psychics say ghosts that are unhappy in death were most likely unhappy in life.

The Grave of Inez Clarke

Cemeteries have long been a favorite location for stories of ghostly happenings. Like ghost stories in general, few of these stories can ever be proved—or disproved. And yet occasionally a story surfaces that is just too good to be true. This was apparently the case with the story of the ghost of a little girl named Inez Clarke of Chicago, Illinois.

Six-year-old Inez is said to have died in 1880 after being struck by lightning while at a family picnic. Devastated by the loss of their daughter, her parents hired a sculptor to create a life-size statue of Inez to mark her

grave at the old Graceland Cemetery. The statue is of Inez wearing her favorite dress, clutching a parasol, and sitting on a stool. Like some other Chicago grave sculptures, Inez's statue was placed in a glass box to protect it from wind and weather.

The statue has attracted a lot of attention over the years, with people leaving flowers and gifts at the grave site even a century after the girl's death. Not surprisingly, the grave has also become known for being haunted. Sometimes strange sounds come from the grave, as though someone is weeping. Other times people have heard a child's voice singing. But the most unnerving of the ghostly activity concerns the statue itself. Some people have said that Inez's statue periodically disappears from its glass box. This takes place, says ghost researcher Troy Taylor, during severe thunderstorms:

> Many years ago, a night watchman for the Pinkerton [detective and security] agency allegedly stated that he was making his rounds one night during a storm and discovered that the box that holds [the statue] was empty. He left the cemetery that night, never to return. Other guards have also reported it missing, only to find it back in place when they pass by again, or the following morning.[23]

A Little Research—and a Big Shock

One researcher decided to dig a little further into the story of Inez Clarke. In 2007 Al Walavich discovered a large hole in the story about her ghost. He learned that no one named Inez Clarke is buried at Graceland Cemetery. Walavich found that no such person had even existed, based

Phantom Chickens?

Chicken Alley in Shawano, Wisconsin, just northwest of Green Bay, is a haunted country road. Ghost researchers Chad Lewis and Terry Fisk describe the goings-on:

"Chicken Alley is a short L-shaped road nestled in the quiet countryside just outside Shawano. Though short, this picturesque country road has been the scene of more than one bizarre occurrence. Witnesses traveling the route have reported spotting several chickens running down the road. But they aren't just any chickens—you can see right through them! Often these chickens vanish into thin air."

Source: Mark Moran and Mark Sceurman, eds., *Weird Hauntings: True Tales of Ghostly Places*. New York: Sterling, 2006, p. 66.

on the dates on the statue's base. "Based on cemetery records," he told the *Chicago Sun-Times*, "there's no such person buried in that grave."[24]

Walavich believes that a Scottish monument maker named Andrew Gage made the statue long ago as an advertisement for his work. He invented the name Inez Clarke for the nonexistent child. And because people do enjoy a ghost story, a legend began about poor Inez. "I confess that I was fooled by the tales that had been recounted and many other writers have been, as well," says Taylor. "Perhaps we all wished a little too hard for this particular Chicago ghost story to be true."[25]

OPPOSITE: The 20th Maine Infantry Regiment fights to hold back the Confederate charge up Little Round Top in the Battle of Gettysburg. After the battle, soldiers on both sides talked of seeing a ghostly figure that resembled George Washington.

"I Could Tell You, Even with My Eyes Closed"

Though many people need no convincing that a cemetery can be haunted, battlefields have an even stronger ghostly reputation. Perhaps, say experts, because so much fear and violent death occurred in so quick a time and on such a large scale, some spirits may be unaware that they have been killed. As a result, they linger in the places where they and their fellow soldiers were killed—sometimes looking for fallen friends, other times, convinced that the battle is still raging.

The most haunted battlefield in the United States is at Gettysburg, Pennsylvania, the site of a bloody three-day battle during the Civil War. When it was over, nearly 8,000 soldiers and 3,000 horses lay dead on the battlefield. Since that time visitors to Gettysburg have often reported sounds of battle. Late at night some people have smelled gunpowder and have heard the shrieks of dying horses. Phantom soldiers wandering the fields, calling out for their brothers-in-arms, have also been reported. According to witnesses, such phantoms are visible for

only a minute or so, then fade and disappear. And other visitors say that while they have not seen ghosts, they experience feelings they have in no other place.

"I've been to Gettysburg several times," says Paul White, a history buff from New York.

It's a remarkable place, and the feelings you get as you walk around are very intense. I always feel incredible sensations of sadness and loss when I'm there. I do know people who say they have seen odd lights at night in the area where the battles took place. I don't disbelieve them. But for me, most of all is the really, really intense feeling. Without knowing I was at Gettysburg, I could tell you, even with my eyes closed. It's not a smell or a temperature or a noise or anything like that. It's just impossible to explain if you've never been there.[26]

Washington at Gettysburg

The sightings of ghosts at Gettysburg even occurred during the battles themselves. One documented incident took place on the third day of fighting, July 3, 1863, when Confederate troops suffered a huge loss. The Union victory that day is said to have changed the course of the entire war. And interestingly, many of the Union soldiers credited their victory to the inspiration they received from a well-known ghostly figure on the battlefield.

That afternoon the 20th Maine Infantry Regiment, commanded by Colonel Joshua Chamberlain, was struggling to hold a position on a piece of higher ground known as Little Round Top. The soldiers were running out of ammunition and had resorted to rummaging through the

cartridge boxes of soldiers lying dead on the ground. The Confederate troops, however, had plenty of ammunition. Things were definitely not looking good for the North.

It seemed that without ammunition, their only option was hand-to-hand combat, and so Colonel Chamberlain began to order his men to fix bayonets on their weapons and charge the Confederate line. At this point, witnesses later said, a ghostly figure appeared, dressed in a vintage uniform from another time in history. According to annals of the International Ghost Hunter Society, an Internet group that compiles stories of hauntings, the troops "watched as it rode along the thin blue line of Federal troops. With every man it passed, soldiers picked up hope and found courage to fight."[27] Some of the Confederate soldiers saw it, too, and shot at it, but bullets seemed to have no effect.

Long after the battle the soldiers spoke openly about how much the ghost looked like paintings they had seen of George Washington. They believed that his spirit could very well have come not only to save them, but in the process, save the union of the nation he had fought to create. Stories of Washington's appearance at Gettysburg even reached the executive branch of the U.S. government. Secretary of war Edwin Stanton ordered an official investigation. Hundreds of men who had fought in that battle—even a high-ranking general named Oliver Hunt—insisted that without a doubt they had seen the ghost of George Washington.

The government's investigation neither proved nor disproved the appearance of George Washington's ghost. But whatever the men saw that day—whether it was truly a ghost or a figment of their imaginations—it gave them the courage to win an improbable victory in a devastating battle.

Ghosts on the Move

Just as with battlefield ghosts, the spirits of people killed in sudden violent accidents are said to linger at the site of their death. Whether it is an automobile accident, a plane crash, or a sunken boat, ghosts are believed to linger. Ghost researchers believe that those killed in traumatic accidents may be unaware that they have died. Their spirits are more apt to roam at the site of the accident, often looking for friends or loved ones. Sometimes they may also try to deal with whatever caused the accident in the first place.

A Horrific Accident in Maco

One of the most famous of these spirits is that of a railroad conductor named Joe Baldwin. He worked on what is now called the Atlantic Coast Railroad, servicing passengers in North Carolina, South Carolina, and Georgia. One night in 1867, a terrible accident occurred near the town of Maco, in the southern part of North Carolina.

Baldwin was riding in the caboose when it unexpectedly coasted to a stop. Alone in the caboose, he looked out the window to see what was going on. He saw that the caboose had become uncoupled from the rest of the train and that a train was coming up, full speed, right behind him.

According to witnesses in the oncoming train, Baldwin grabbed a lantern and began swinging it back and

Flames rise from the wreckage of an airplane that crashed in New York in 2009. Some believe that the spirits of those killed in violent accidents such as plane crashes linger, perhaps searching for loved ones.

forth from the back of the caboose in hope of alerting the train to his presence on the tracks. The witnesses said that Baldwin continued to swing the lantern, even when it was clear that the train was going too fast to stop. Baldwin was killed immediately—crushed by the impact.

Witnessed by a President

It was only days after the collision, just after Baldwin's funeral, that the first sightings of a mysterious light began. People who lived near the tracks reported that the light swung back and forth, in the same movement a trainman might use, in the same spot on the track where Baldwin was killed. According to local historians, no explanation could be found for the light, which eventually came to be known as the "Maco light."

Several years later, as the light continued, railroad officials decided something had to be done. Too many trains were seeing the light and slowing down, thinking it warned of a problem on the tracks. But when they would get to the light, they realized nothing was there—no person, no lantern, and no problem. Beginning in the 1870s the railroad began using two signal lanterns—one red and one green (as differentiated from Maco's white lantern light)—to warn of a problem on the tracks. From that point on, engineers knew not to stop for the Maco light.

The mysterious light became well-known in the area and was even witnessed by a president. In 1889 Grover Cleveland was traveling by train along the Atlantic Coast line and asked about the strange light. He was told the story and found it fascinating. According to historian Valerie Robertson, "He carried the story back with him to Washington, D.C., spurring national attention for the tale."[28]

Searching for Explanations

As years went by, the light continued to fascinate scientists as well as ghost researchers, and there was no shortage of theories. Some wondered whether it was a reflection caused by automobile headlights. But when the light was first noticed, the automobile had not yet been invented. Still, authorities tried an experiment: For several nights they halted all automobile traffic in the area at night to see whether that made a difference, but the light still appeared. Naturalists from the Smithsonian Institution came to investigate, thinking at first that the light might be caused by heat lightning. However, those scientists changed their minds, for the amount of light caused by heat lightning is not as bright as the Maco light. With experts' inability to find a reasonable explanation, the best theory seemed to be that it was Joe Baldwin's spirit continuing to wave the lantern, hoping that this time, he might prevent the accident.

In 1977 the section of track where Joe Baldwin was killed was replaced, and the sightings stopped. But people in Maco have strong memories of the phenomenon. For years afterward, people continued go out to the site at night in hope of seeing the light. Brooks Preik remembers driving to Maco with her family to get a good look. At first nothing was there, she recalls. Her husband got out of the car and began walking the tracks. "All of a sudden we all saw it," she says. "All of a sudden all of us were aware of it at the same time. You could hear the gasp going through the group."[29]

Ghosts of Flight 191

A more recent accident that appears to have produced many lingering spirits was the crash of American Airlines Flight 191 on May 25, 1979. It was a deadly crash—291

passengers and crew died along with 2 people on the ground. From the outset, no one seemed to be worried about the flight. The crew was very experienced, and the plane had logged thousands of hours of trouble-free flying. The day was sunny and clear and seemed perfect for the nonstop flight between Chicago and Los Angeles. But everything changed as the plane began its takeoff at O'Hare International Airport.

As it sped down the runway, one of the plane's engines began coming loose, falling away from the plane. As the plane climbed into the air, the loose engine crashed down onto the runway. Within seconds, the plane fell to earth in a fiery crash as it hit an abandoned airplane hangar a half mile from the airport.

Odd Lights, Knocking Doors

As happens with every airline accident, transportation safety experts began analyzing the cause of the crash. As the investigation progressed, another mystery was unfolding on the ground. By August, less than two months after the crash of Flight 191, dozens of people were reporting strange occurrences near the crash site.

Some reported hearing moans and screams coming from the field where the plane went down. When they looked at the field, they saw no one. People also reported seeing unexplained white lights shining on the field. Motorists driving on a nearby road told police that the lights flickered and bobbed. "First thought to be flashlights carried by ghoulish souvenir hunters," writes researcher Troy Taylor, "officers responded to the reports to find the field was silent and deserted. No one was ever found, despite patrols arriving on the scene almost moments after receiving a report."[30]

Even stranger, were the experiences of people liv-

Did You Know?
One of the most often-seen ghosts in Chicago is Resurrection Mary, the spirit of a young woman who was killed in a traffic accident in the 1930s.

ing in a nearby mobile home park. Many of the mobile home park residents were police and firefighters, and they said they heard knocking on their doors and windows but found no one there. In some cases residents heard footsteps clanging on the metal stairs of the trailers, as well as doorknobs being turned. Dogs at the park were normally fairly quiet, but they began barking endlessly at the empty field—as though they could sense the presence of someone that no one could see.

Visible Spirits?

Invisible strangers are creepy enough, but those who actually appeared at people's homes near the crash sight were even scarier. People were reported to have come to the door of residents at night, frantic because they could not find their luggage or because they had to make a connection to another flight and did not know how. After talking a moment, the stranger would turn and walk into the dark.

Even though nearly three decades have passed since the crash, the ghostly activity seems to have continued. According to one researcher, a man walking his dog one night many years after the crash had an eerie experience:

> He was approached by a young man who explained that he needed to make an emergency telephone call. The man with his dog looked at this person curiously, for he seemed to reek of gasoline and also appeared to be smoldering. At first, he just assumed the man had been running on this chilly night and steam was coming from his clothing, but when he turned away to

Did You Know?
Two crewmen aboard the oil tanker *S.S. Watertown* were killed and buried at sea in 1924. For days, the faces of the men appeared in the water of the ship's wake and were seen by the entire crew.

point out a nearby phone and turned back again—the man had vanished![31]

So far, no one has been able to explain any of the sightings, from the bobbing lights to the strange people walking around the site of the crash. Even as recently as 2007—28 years after the crash—mysterious individuals have been reported to have stopped passers-by or approached nearby houses to ask an airline-related question, and then apparently vanished afterward.

Ships That Haunt

Ghost sightings are also a common feature of shipwrecks. Often, the ghosts associated with these events are not the spirits of the crew or passengers but of the ships themselves. One of the most famous of these ships was the *HMS Eurydice*, a three-masted, 26-gun British warship, that capsized in 1878.

The ship hit a fluke storm during a warm spring day in March 1878. An immense storm cloud suddenly overtook the ship as it sailed past the mountainous Isle of Wight in the English Channel. Only at the last minute did the crew realize the danger. By that time they were in deep trouble. The icy spray hit the *Eurydice* like a punch, and though the crew struggled to keep the ship afloat, in less than a half hour, it capsized. Of the 360-man crew, only 2 survived.

Perhaps because of the *Eurydice*'s violent and sudden end, it's ghost seems to linger, haunting that portion of the English Channel. Sailors for more than a century have claimed that they have seen the ship during rainy nights at sea, its sails flying. And visitors to the Isle of Wight have reported seeing the easily recognized form of a nineteenth-century warship even during the day.

Did You Know?
Many ghost legends report that ghosts love the smell of lemons.

The DC-10 aircraft that was American Airlines Flight 191 burns as firefighters try to douse the flames. After the accident, many strange occurrences were reported near the crash site, including moans, screams, and flickering lights.

Robin Ford, a retired teacher, says he saw the ship while he was having a barbecue on the beach with friends. "It moved slowly towards the shore," he says, "then it just seemed to up-end and slipped silently out of view."[32]

A Royal Testimony

The most well-known witness to the ghost ship *Eurydice* was Britain's Prince Edward. In 1998 he was the host of a BBC television series called *Crown and Country*, which dealt with the history of England, and he and his TV crew were on the Isle of Wight in May 1998. He later explained that he was telling the crew about the ship and what had happened to it.

"We were talking about a ghost ship on the Isle of Wight," he said, "and how we could illustrate this three-masted schooner that just disappears. Suddenly someone said, 'Look, there's one now,' and sure enough, out to sea there was a three-masted schooner."[33]

The director of the program said later that they were delighted to see such a ship, for it meant that they would be able to save the cost of paying to rent one for the shot. At the time, he later said, he thought it was simply a replica of a nineteenth-century vessel—perhaps used in the making of films. "Like the rest of us, Edward was pleased at our stroke of luck at seeing it, because it saved us time and money getting footage of something similar."[34]

"There Is Something Definitely Out There"

The camera crew shot some footage, but decided to wait until the ship got closer to shore before they shot more. However, a few minutes later, it seemed that the ship had simply vanished. "We . . . took our eyes off it for a few minutes, but when we went to film it again," said the director, "it had gone."[35]

Racing the Train

Dozens of train conductors, engineers, construction crews, and railroad passengers have reported seeing a strange sight as they ride through North Dakota, South Dakota, and Wyoming—a Sioux Indian in war paint, riding a beautiful black horse, chasing the train. A salesman who used to travel through that part of the country frequently says he has seen the ghost five or six times in different parts of the Dakotas. "[The horse and rider] seem to be solid flesh," he says, "but there's a kind of shimmering around them. It's like watching a strip of really old movie film being projected onto the prairie."

Source: Quoted in Brad Steiger, *Real Ghosts, Restless Spirits, and Haunted Places.* Canton, MI: Visible Ink, 2003, p. 407.

The whole thing seemed bizarre to the crew and Edward. They could find absolutely no explanation for how it could have disappeared in so short a time, especially since it was headed directly toward the shore. The next day they tried to trace the ship to find out where it had gone. However, neither naval authorities nor the Sail Training Association had any idea. The only three-masted schooners in existence were far from the Isle of Wight that day.

Had they actually seen the ghost ship *Eurydice*? Prince Edward does not dismiss the idea. "I am quite convinced as far as ghosts are concerned," he says, "that there are too many stories, coincidences, occurrences and strange stories. There is something definitely out there, but what it is I don't really know."[36]

While hosting a television series about English history, Prince Edward (pictured) visited the Isle of Wight with his crew. While there, they witnessed an unexplainable event: the appearance—and disappearance—of a ship that closely resembled the ghost ship *Eurydice*.

The Dead Zone

Roads and highways are other common sites of hauntings. Ghost researchers believe that some of the ghosts that haunt roadsides belong to people who experienced swift and violent deaths. They believe that these ghosts are confused about whether they are alive or dead. However, not all ghosts who haunt roadways were victims of accidents.

On one patch of Florida's Interstate 4 between Orlando and Tampa, the ghosts are not believed to be victims of a crash but of the road itself.

This segment of highway, known to local residents as "the Dead Zone," is about one-quarter-mile long, and in-

cludes an overpass just north of Orlando. Since 1960 this area of highway has been the site of more than 2,000 accidents—more than the total number of accidents on the rest of the highway—including the busy exchanges around Tampa.

The cause of the accidents may be ghosts—the spirits of a family buried on that site back in the 1880s. The parents and their two children were part of a settlement of St. Joseph's Catholic Colony and died during a yellow fever epidemic. According to researcher Charlie Carlson, the graves were supposed to be removed during construction of the interstate. But that did not happen.

"They [the graves] are still there," he says. "In fact, when I-4 came through in 1960, the graves were roped off and marked for removal [and for placement in a new site], but they never removed the graves. Instead they dumped fill dirt on top to elevate the new highway."[37]

"I Heard the Truck Driver Calling My Name"
Ever since the highway opened, along that stretch motorists have reported cell phones and radios that do not work and odd lights floating above the roadbed. In some cases, ghostly figures have been spotted. That is what happened to a New York driver named Christine, who knew nothing of the legend of the Dead Zone—but is now a believer in ghosts.

Her experience occurred one summer afternoon in 2002, when her car broke down on I-4. She coasted to a stop on an overpass. The railing along the bridge was short, and it was very difficult for her to cross the bridge on foot. "I'm so afraid of heights," she explains, "I was afraid to cross it with all the cars speeding by."[38]

Halfway across, she became really afraid, and, worried that she would fall over the railing, she froze. All of a

Sheriff's deputies and others examine the site of a fatal car crash. One section of Florida's Interstate 4 is known for its many car crashes. Researchers believe that a ghost family buried beneath the highway may somehow be responsible.

sudden, a big silver and white refrigerated truck pulled off the road just past the bridge. "I heard the truck driver calling my name—strange, because I have no idea how he knew it," she remembers. "He kept telling me to walk toward him and not to look down."[39]

The Ghost Driver

She did as he asked and walked slowly toward the driver, who then offered to give her a lift to the next exit. Even now she recalls how clean the truck looked, especially the cab. "It was like brand new inside," she says. "I mean just spick and span. The only thing in it was a clipboard that, strangely enough, didn't have any papers."[40]

When the truck driver pulled into the closest gas station, Christine climbed out, and as she walked inside the station, she noticed that she did not hear the truck running at all. "I turned to look, and the truck was gone," she remembers. "There was a man sitting on a bench in front of the store and I asked him if he had seen the truck that was there. He gave me a puzzled look and said 'I've been sitting here all morning, and haven't seen any trucks pull in.'"[41]

Christine's experience is believed to be tied to the Dead Zone. The very first fatal crash on this section of the I-4 occurred when a silver and white refrigerated semi jackknifed, killing the driver. Though the family of spirits from the 1800s may have caused the accident, some say Christine's friendly truck driver may very well have been the ghost of that driver. Whether or not he was a ghost, many wonder if the frequency of accidents and odd occurrences within the Dead Zone is a reminder of the restlessness of the bodies buried beneath.

Did You Know?
Before the attacks on September 11, 2001, the crash of Flight 191 was the worst airline disaster in U.S. history.

Ghosts Inside

Ghosts can linger and haunt in almost any setting. However, most ghosts' haunts throughout the centuries have been buildings—jails, theaters, offices, restaurants, and especially houses. Ghost researchers say that although these sites are not necessarily the places where violent, sudden deaths occurred, they are filled with many years' worth of energy and emotion. When people who stayed in these buildings die, their spirits often seem closely tied to these places.

Cell Number 10

Reports of jail and prison hauntings are incredibly numerous—not just in the United States but throughout the world. The old prison in Invernay, Scotland, is a good example. The prison was in use in the early and mid-1800s, housing more than 6,000 prisoners during that time.

As with many old prisons, the conditions at Invernay were deplorable. The prison had neither toilet facilities nor heat. Food was sparse and often rancid. Prisoners were often beaten and tortured. Children as young as 10 were imprisoned there for crimes such as stealing a potato from a farmer or a bit of cheese from a market stall. And because of overcrowded conditions, these children often shared their cells with adult criminals who were guilty of violent crimes such as murder and rape. Some

people suggest that the terrible conditions have left behind negative energy that can still be felt there today.

Writer Janet Brennan visited the prison-turned-museum in 2006. She had read that the prison was known to be haunted, and she was curious to see for herself. She later reported that as she walked through the hallway of cells, she definitely could sense something strange outside one of them. "I felt a fluttering in my heart," she wrote. "It was similar to the feeling of butterflies in the stomach, but in my chest. I've never experienced this feeling before."[42]

According to the warden who oversees the museum, once when the building was empty a tape recorder left on in one of the cells had picked up a voice saying, "Get out!" In addition, service animals such as guide dogs for the blind almost always refuse to walk past the cell, as if they sense danger. Some workers have heard mumblings in that particular cell, especially at night.

A Haunted Courthouse?

Another government building, this one in Santa Fe, New Mexico, was believed to be haunted – at least for about a week. A security camera at the city's courthouse captured images around the entrances to the building. Early on the morning of June 15, 2007, the videotape revealed what appeared to be a ghost—a glowing blob that seemed to hover next to the front entrance.

Some people thought it could be the ghost of a man who had been murdered. Someone suggested that it could be the spirit of a woman who had been killed by her boyfriend after judges at the courthouse would not issue a restraining order against him. Others thought it was likely the lights of passing cars. The story spread when the "ghost video" appeared on YouTube.

Did You Know?
Sarah Winchester, heir to the Winchester rifle fortune, believed that her California house was haunted. She spent 37 years of her life adding on rooms to the house to appease the angry ghosts—victims of the rifles that bore her name.

Paranormal investigator Benjamin Radford was called in and dismissed the car light explanation. The lights of passing cars would be moving, not hovering in one place as did the glowing blob. But he was intrigued by the cottonwood trees nearby and wondered if the large glowing blob was actually something tiny that was close to the camera lens.

He arrived the next morning at the same time the blob had appeared the week before and placed a few insects he had gathered from the trees onto the camera. "I waited for them to crawl around, and soon went inside the courthouse to check the videotape," Radford later explained. "While some of the insects [such as ladybugs] were too large and dark to be the ghostly culprit, at 7:26 A.M., we hit pay dirt."[43] What had looked very much like something large and glowing was a very small bug that had wandered onto the camera lens.

Haunting the Stage

Some ghost researchers believe that theaters can be some of the most haunted structures. Perhaps, they say, it is because the intense emotions played out on stage—as well as the nervousness and exhilaration of performing actors—attract restless spirits. Whatever the cause, for hundreds of years actors and crews throughout the world have reported seeing ghosts of people haunting the theaters where they once worked.

One of the most-witnessed modern theater ghosts does not belong to an actor or director but to an usher. In the mid-1960s, teenager Richard Miller worked as an usher at the famous Guthrie Theater in Minneapolis. When he turned 18, he began attending the nearby University of Minnesota, but he was shy and seemed to have trouble making friends. On Saturday, February 5, 1967, Miller

Did You Know?
More than one ghost haunts the White House. Many people have heard Thomas Jefferson practicing his violin in the Yellow Oval Room.

made the decision to end his life. Wearing his usher uniform, he went into a store and bought a pistol and some ammunition. He then shot and killed himself while sitting in his car in the store's parking lot.

Soon after his death, Guthrie management began getting complaints from theatergoers. It seemed that during performances an usher would rudely walk up and down the aisle and stare at them. Asked if they could identify the young man they saw, the patrons provided a description that matched Richard Miller exactly—down to the birthmark on his cheek.

The Guthrie Theater in Minneapolis was haunted for nearly three decades by a young man who killed himself while working as an usher there. The ghost disappeared after an exorcism, and did not resurface even after the theater was rebuilt at a new site (pictured).

Sightings of Miller continued for almost 30 years. Not only did theater patrons see him, but staff members who knew him personally reported seeing him. He walked around various parts of the theater but spent most of his time haunting Row 18, the area to which he was most frequently assigned. Finally, in 1994 the theater arranged an exorcism—a religious ceremony conducted by priests to rid a place of ghosts. After that, Miller's spirit seemed to have left the Guthrie. Even after the theater was rebuilt at a different site, the former usher's ghost has remained silent.

Did You Know?
Ghosts are reported to haunt schools in all 50 states.

"That's a Strange House You've Got There, Mate"

While hauntings can occur almost anywhere, the most frequently cited indoor locations for ghosts are houses. The emotions experienced in most people's homes are almost certainly not as frightening as those felt in a prison or on a battlefield. But strong emotions, both positive and negative, occur for years—sometimes even over a lifetime. And if some ghost researchers are correct in their theory that many spirits linger because of the presence of those emotions, then it is no wonder that houses attract ghosts.

The actor Richard Harris, who played—among many other roles—Professor Dumbledore in the first two Harry Potter movies, lived in a haunted house for years. In the 1960s, early in his acting career, Harris found an interesting old house in London and immediately bought it.

The first thing Harris did after that was to ask a friend who had once been a burglar to inspect it. Harris wanted no break-ins at his new home and was sure that a former burglar would be able to spot any weaknesses in the security of the house. But what the ex-burglar found was more complicated than any security breach.

Harris's friend did a quick walk-through of the house one evening and was startled to hear what sounded very much like a child crying. The house should have been empty, and the man wondered if somehow a child had wandered inside during the day and was unable to find his or her way out. As he walked up the stairs, the crying became louder. It was clear that it was a child, and whoever it was sounded very distraught.

But when he entered the room, which was upstairs in the tower of the old house, he saw no one. The room was empty, and the crying had stopped. Rattled, Harris's friend went back downstairs and found Harris. He gave the actor a few tips on beefing up the house's security, and added, "But that's a strange house you've got there, mate."[44]

Actor Richard Harris, who played Professor Dumbledore in the first two Harry Potter movies, lived for many years in a haunted house in London. The sounds of ghostly activity included crying and the slamming of doors.

A Noisy Ghost

Harris rather liked the idea of owning a haunted house. He decided to find out more about the house and who had lived there before him. He learned that many years before, an eight-year-old boy had been buried under the tower of the house. Assuming the ghost was the spirit of

that child, Harris resolved that he would find a way to share the house with the ghost.

He soon found out that sharing a house with a ghost is not always easy. The ghost often woke Harris up in the middle of the night by running up and down the tower stairs and slamming doors. Harris tried to explain to the young ghost that actors needed plenty of sleep. Harris told one interviewer that he warned the ghost to "stop making all the late-night ruckus" or he "would have him exorcised!"[45]

Did You Know?
Ghosts at the Tower of London, many without heads, have haunted the structure since 1241.

Over the years, Harris said that he and the ghost learned to get along with one another. He frequently voiced his regret at having to be away from the house when on location for a movie because he found that he missed the ghost. But he had to work, he said, and not just for his own sake. "I have to make buckets of money just to support my haunted house and its noisy little ghost,"[46] he once told an interviewer.

The Most Famous Haunted House

Another not-so-scary ghost resides in the White House—though many people do not realize that the place is haunted. And while a number of unidentified spirits have walked those halls at night, the most famous ghost is very recognizable—that of Abraham Lincoln. Lincoln's ghost has been seen by many in the White House—visitors and residents alike.

The greatest number of sightings have taken place in the room that served as Lincoln's study. It is now known as the Lincoln bedroom. It was an important place for Lincoln, for he made many Civil War decisions, as well as signed, the Emancipation Proclamation there. However, in the years since then, guests who have slept in that room have reported strange feelings, such as cold spots

The ghost of Abraham Lincoln is just one of many spirits that have been spotted roaming the White House (pictured). First Lady Eleanor Roosevelt claimed she often felt Lincoln's presence in her study.

and odd sensations that someone is in the room with them. A White House clerk saw Lincoln sitting on the edge of the bed in that room, pulling off his black boots. President Ronald Reagan once told reporters his dog Rex "would start down that long hall toward that room just glaring as if he's seeing something, and barking, and he stops in front of Lincoln's door, the bedroom door."[47]

Lincoln's ghost seemed to be most active during the years that Franklin D. Roosevelt was president.

Roosevelt's wife, Eleanor, often used the Lincoln bedroom as a study, and though she said she never saw him, she often felt his presence. The most vivid sighting was by Queen Wilhelmina of the Netherlands, who in 1945 accepted an offer to stay overnight at the White House. She was in the Lincoln bedroom when she heard a knock at her door late that night. When she opened it, she saw Lincoln dressed in a top hat and dress coat. It is said that the queen promptly fainted.

The Old Slave House

While Lincoln's ghost and that of the boy who haunted Richard Harris's home were not frightening, many of the ghosts haunting houses throughout the world are. One of the most frightening of America's haunted houses is located in Equality, Illinois, a small town located on the Illinois-Kentucky border. The original name of the house is Hickory Hill, but most people today know it as the Old Slave House.

The house was built by John Crenshaw in the early 1800s. Crenshaw owned many acres of land with huge salt deposits that he mined. In the nineteenth century, salt was extremely valuable, both as a food preservative and as currency for purchasing goods. Laboring in a salt mine was very hard and unpleasant, and it was difficult for Crenshaw to keep workers. And since slavery was illegal in Illinois, he could not use slave labor.

So Crenshaw devised a plan to make sure he always had a workforce. He paid men called "night riders" to ride through the countryside at night and capture runaway slaves who had come up from nearby Kentucky (a slave state). Crenshaw kept some of the captured slaves to work in his salt mines so that he did not have to pay them a wage.

Ghost Lights

Theater people are among the biggest believers in ghosts. Many believe that the energy and ranges of emotion played out on stages around the world create a perfect atmosphere for hauntings. In Shakespeare's time, theater owners kept a candle lit at night after everyone left, to keep evil spirits from haunting the stage. Today, almost all theaters keep a single light bulb above the stage lit for the same reason. It is called a ghost light.

Hickory Hill was built with Crenshaw's illegal slave business in mind. When they were not working, the slaves were kept as prisoners in the house. The attic was divided into 12 cell-like rooms with barred windows. Each cell was so tiny that an adult could hardly turn around within it. In addition to keeping them in deplorable conditions, Crenshaw beat and whipped the slaves. And because Crenshaw was a pillar within the

Cold spots, rattling chains, and sobbing have been reported in the Old Slave House (pictured), built in Illinois in the 1800s. Residents in the house included captured runaway slaves who were often chained in tiny cells.

community—and especially the church—almost no one knew what went on at Hickory Hill.

"I Never Believed in Ghosts Before"

In the years since the end of the Civil War, the stories of the slave trade at Hickory Hill have become known. In recent years visitors have been able to tour the house, and they have had some interesting reactions. Many have

reported feeling cold spots in the attic and hearing the sounds of rattling chains. More than a few residents have heard moans and sobbing from the attic late at night.

David, a university professor in Chicago, decided to tour the house as he drove back home from a trip to southern Illinois. He says that he was the only visitor that day, and at first he decided to take his time going through the place—until he reached the attic:

> The whole time I was up there [in the attic], I was sure that someone was there with me. I was constantly turning around to see who was behind me, but there was never anyone there. Finally I became so unnerved that I left the house and walked out to my car. It was parked in the gravel lot directly in front, and when I reached it, I looked up at the attic window. I clearly saw a face looking out at me, even though I knew no one had been in the house![48]

Did You Know?
Two-thirds of British citizens polled say they believe in ghosts.

David went back inside and asked the owner if someone else had come in, but he was told that no one had. "I still have no explanation for what happened," he told ghost researcher Taylor. "I never believed in ghosts before that, and while I'm still not sure that I do, I just have no explanation for what I saw in that window."[49]

The Old Slave House was closed in 1996 because of the declining health of its owners. However, Illinois officials have said they plan to re-open the house as a state historic site. Ghost hunters and others interested in the house's history remain curious about whether the ghostly activity will remain.

Good-Bye to Haunting Spirits

People who have experienced what seem to be ghostly activities are usually eager to put a stop to them as quickly as possible. The idea that a restless, angry, or uneasy spirit is roaming through their homes or offices is unsettling. But exactly what can people do to put a stop to it?

Eliminating the Not-So-Ghostly

Calling a ghost research group is a good first step. Sometimes called "ghost hunters," these groups specialize in getting to the cause of what seems to be paranormal, or seemingly unexplainable, events. But before a case is categorized as a haunting, most ghost hunters will carefully examine all aspects of a location to see if they can find a less dramatic explanation for the mysterious events.

Experts say that it is very important to consider all possibilities when trying to get to the bottom of strange activity. In fact, says researcher Grace Donne, most experts consider the best ghost hunters to be those groups that do not begin with the conclusion that the structure is haunted.

"I compare the situation to going to a doctor because you are always tired and lack energy," she says. "A good doctor would look at the most likely causes, like maybe that you're not getting enough sleep at night, or you aren't eating right—and eliminate those possibilities first. On the other hand, it would be silly for a doctor to start

out with the idea that you have a rare sleeping disorder. The chances are, that kind of thinking is a waste of time."[50]

"It's the 5 Percent That Keeps Us Interested"

Therefore, when a homeowner is concerned that a ghost might be in the attic because of odd noises coming from upstairs, it is important to first look at the boring but far more likely causes, such as a family of mice or old creaky floorboards. Danny Owen, who is part of a Kentucky ghost-hunting team, says that 95 percent or more of the time, the cause of the activity can be easily explained.

Owen goes to supposedly haunted locations with a level, a tape measure, and a carpenter's square in his hands. "My job is to go in and make sure the floors are level and the doors hung straight," he says. "The group looks for obvious explanations for things that go bump, such as loose windows, crookedly hung doors, and unbalanced furniture."[51]

That kind of research often provides an explanation less frightening than ghosts. In 2003 police department employees in Shelbyville, Kentucky, were convinced that their offices were haunted. Some of the weird occurrences were a desk drawer that opened by itself and sudden, unexplained variances in temperature in sections of the building.

Owen quickly discovered that the desk drawer was simply off-kilter and thus could slide open by itself. In addition, the thermostat was broken and as a result, it kept resetting itself. By fixing those things, much of the "haunting" could be explained. That does not mean that ghostly activity never exists in houses, however. Owen and his team get far more excited once they realize that some things cannot be explained as plumbing, carpentry,

Did You Know?
Exorcists who are dealing with evil ghosts often stand inside a circle of salt during the ceremony. Salt is believed to keep demons away.

or electrical problems. "It's the 5 percent [of cases] that keeps us interested,"[52] he says.

Going to the Next Level

While part of the team looks for possible structural explanations, other members do research on the house. They look at local records to find out the house's history since it was built. They make a list of the various owners and then check old newspaper records to learn of any noteworthy events that may have occurred—deaths, suicides, accidents, or anything else that might point to a possible reason for a spirit to haunt the home.

After compiling a list of owners and events, members of the ghost-hunting team conduct as many interviews as possible. They contact former owners or renters of the house, as well as neighbors. By interviewing these people, the researchers can collect more specific information about any events that might have occurred at, or in, the house.

"Just knowing that neighbors have seen odd things once in a while can give credence to a homeowner's story," says Gary Jensen, a Minnesota ghost hunter.

> We had a case . . . when a man—an older guy who was new to the neighborhood— was insisting he was seeing large, reddish-gold lights near [one of] his trees at night. We weren't sure how accurate his description of the lights was, because of his age.
>
> We talked to neighbors who might have had a view of the tree at night, and were lucky. We found one guy our homeowner hadn't met yet, who said that yeah, he'd seen that same odd light. The neighbor said he and his

"One of the Eeriest Things I've Ever Heard"

Elle, a ghost hunter, believes that she inadvertently recorded the voice of a ghost named Dave in the summer of 2007.

We were going through this old building in St. Paul that is believed to be haunted. We often take a tape recorder so we can talk and record what we say—that way we don't have to worry about writing our impressions down. But that night, when we were making notes from our recording, we heard a man's voice saying, "I'm Dave, I'm okay. I'm okay."

It made no sense. There was no one else there that day, and all of us were women, so it clearly was not one of our voices. It was a brand new tape—there was no way anything else had been recorded on it. It was one of the eeriest things I've ever heard.

Source: Elle, personal interview, November 19, 2008, Minneapolis, Minnesota.

wife used to call it Tinkerbell, because it kind of darted around like the cartoon character. They never figured it out, but they'd seen it maybe fifty or sixty times over the twenty years they'd lived there, and their description backed up our client. Plus it pointed out that the event had occurred when several others had owned the home.[53]

Jensen says that though they never solved that case, they eliminated every possible explanation they could—which pointed to the likelihood of a paranormal event. "We crossed off bugs, reflections, anything you could think of, but we got nowhere," he says. "But having gotten a good description like that from the neighbor made a huge difference for us. Although it's on our records as 'unsolved,' that case showed us the importance of talking to other potential witnesses, just in case."[54]

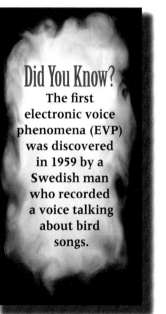

Tools for Validating a Ghost

Once it seems to ghost hunters that they have exhausted alternate explanations, they can get serious about trying to prove the presence of a ghost. A number of important tools can help them to do this, and a good ghost-hunting team carries all of them.

For example, a thermometer can enable the ghost hunter to document cold spots in a room. "It's common to experience cold areas in supposedly haunted spaces," says ghost researcher Elle.

But it is helpful to be able to document exactly the variance of temperatures. I use a thermometer that can just be pointed at a small area, and then, when I pull the trig-

ger, it gives me a quick reading. I've had an experience where the homeowner and I both witnessed light orbs in a certain area of the guest bedroom where a lot of the haunting had taken place, and the thermometer showed that the area where the orbs were was almost 30 degrees colder than the room temperature.[55]

Another valuable tool is also one of the least understood—the electromagnetic frequency (EMF) meter, or gauss meter. The EMF meter is used by electricians to locate unsafe or bad wiring; however, ghost hunters say that the meter can have another use.

Because spirits are believed to change the electromagnetic frequency in an area, the meter may indicate the presence of a ghost within an enclosed structure. The EMF meter measures electromagnetic frequency in units called milligauss (mG). A reading of between 1 and 2 mG is normal; however, ghost hunters say that areas where a lot of paranormal activity occurs tend to have EMF readings as high as 7 or 8 mG, although no one is sure why.

"Nothing Beats a Photograph"

Thermometers and meters supply hard data, but these data do not confirm the presence of a ghost. This information only supports the idea that there could be a ghost in the house. What ghost hunters really hope for is to capture some real proof—an image or a sound—of a spirit. Says Gary Jensen, "A good photograph is the gold standard in our line of work. They're rare, but we're always hoping."[56]

Ghost hunters say that people are often confused about what a video camera or a regular still camera could show

that they cannot see when at a haunted site. After all, does a camera not simply capture what the human eye sees? But as ghost hunter Joshua P. Warren explains, a camera can actually see more than the eye can see: "Cameras can reveal things that the naked eye cannot see. For example, when a fan is on, the blades move so fast that you can't see them with the naked eye. But when you photograph them using the proper shutter speed, they appear. Some of these ghostly manifestations may usually move, or oscillate, at a rate too fast for our brains to perceive."[57]

Photographs often surprise the ghost hunter with images that were not noticed at the time. Sometimes roundish lights, or orbs, can be seen floating in an area of the room. Occasionally ghost hunters are startled when a filmy form of a person is revealed in a room where they themselves had noticed nothing. If the form is recognizable at all, say researchers, it could provide clues as to who is doing the haunting—information that can be valuable later when trying to get the ghost to leave.

By themselves, photographs are not necessarily proof of a ghostly presence either. Many photos that purport to show ghosts are murky and the images unclear. Other explanations can sometimes be found for orbs of light, including dust on the camera lens or a reflection. Some ghost researchers have even been known to doctor a photograph, and computer technology now makes that easier than ever.

Ghost Voices
Another highly valued—but controversial—piece of evidence is a voice recording. Since the invention of portable tape recorders, researchers have picked up voices in haunted areas without even trying. They do not hear it at the time, but when the tape is played back they some-

Did You Know?
Ghost hunters have recorded cold spots 50 degrees colder than the room temperature.

times hear a voice. It is a mystery known as EVP, or electronic voice phenomena. EVP has been heard by ghost researchers throughout the world.

No one is certain how EVP works. Some experts have suggested that EVPs are imprints—energy that has been somehow "recorded" in the environment where ghostly activity occurs. Some researchers believe that when situations are right, such as having a particular level of electricity or humidity in the air, the voices can replay. Imprint voices do not respond to the living—they are merely mysterious recordings of voices from the past.

Some EVPs are responsive, however. EVP experts Tom and Lisa Butler recount the experience of a man named David, who was doing some research by leaving his tape recorder running in a supposedly haunted area. After having no luck getting any EVPs, David asked, "Is there any friendly entity that wishes to speak?" He left the tape recorder running, and when he played it back later, a voice asked, "Did anybody answer?"[58]

Though many examples of responsive EVPs exist, they arouse as much skepticism as do ghost photographs. The recordings are rarely clear, and listeners' interpretations of what, if anything, is being said usually differ. And as with photos, recordings can also be altered. Despite the doubts, EVPs are viewed by ghost researchers as one more indication that a place could be haunted.

Did You Know?
The first ghost photography was done by William Mumler in the late 1800s, though many today consider his photos to be fakes.

Saying Good-Bye to a Ghost

Once it seems reasonably certain that a spirit is haunting a structure, various options are available to the owner. Although some homeowners, such as actor Richard Harris, have not been intimidated by the presence of a ghost, the vast majority of people who experience hauntings are. They prefer to have the ghost leave, but often feel helpless

in accomplishing that. Ghost hunters say that people can get rid of a ghost in several ways.

Exorcism, a word which means "casting out," is one way. For centuries, the Roman Catholic Church has had a special rite of exorcism. Originally, the rite of exorcism was used to drive out demons or evil spirits from people. Since 2000, the Catholic Church has allowed certain priests to do exorcisms when evil or destructive spirits seem to be inhabiting a house, though they are not done very often.

But it is not just the Roman Catholic Church that performs exorcisms on houses. In recent years a number of other religions have recognized exorcisms as an important tool in ridding homes of ghosts. The Reverend Donald Beery of the Universal Life Church in California has performed a number of exorcisms. Beery believes that ghosts are forms of energy that remain when people die. "If the person spent their life being mean and evil," he explains, "when they die it is possible that evil can take a psychic form of a ghost."[59]

"There Was a Ghost Living in That House"

In a recent case, a young couple contacted Beery because they had just moved into a house that they felt was haunted. It did not take Beery long, he says, to understand what they meant. "There were a lot of strange happenings," he says, "like ghostly apparitions going through the house, pictures falling off the wall. . . . There was a ghost living in that house."[60]

To perform this exorcism, Beery borrowed a ceremony used for centuries by Native American holy persons. He fashioned what is called a smudge stick, a bundle of sweet grass and sage. After burning the end of it, he used the stick to mark each room as he concentrated on cleansing it of evil spirits.

A Roman Catholic priest takes notes during a Vatican-sponsored course on Satanism, black magic, and exorcism. Exorcism is the most well known way to get rid of a ghost.

Beery says that he went from room to room in a pattern, gradually working his way to the front door, where he and the homeowners chased the ghost out. In this case, the ghost left. "[The couple] didn't have trouble after that,"[61] says Beery.

"It Sounds Very Silly"

Exorcism is not the only way of getting rid of a ghost. Another approach is to simply ask the ghost to leave. Experts say this works a fair amount of the time, but more

successfully if a psychic does it. Psychics are people who have an ability to sense or even to see spirits and can often communicate with them.

Jill, who asks that her last name not be used, contacted a psychic when ghost hunters found no explanation for the whispering she heard throughout her house at night. "She [the psychic] could actually see the ghosts," says Jill. "It sounds very silly, and I know exactly what people will think. But she was very matter-of-fact about it. She told us we had three women ghosts, and they had lived in this house many years ago, and did not want to leave."[62]

Jill says that the psychic spent two days and part of an evening reasoning with the spirits.

> She'd close her eyes, like she was praying, and she'd speak quietly. Then she'd look at them, I guess, and keep repeating "Jill lives here now, and her children. And they don't want to be frightened." Eventually, it worked. It wasn't a real dramatic thing. We did burn incense, because I guess that helps. But it worked. It's been more than eight months and the whispering has stopped.[63]

"Ghosts Are Like Cats"

Karl Petry is a psychic who lives and works in New Jersey. He says he thinks of his ability as a means not only to help frightened or worried homeowners but to bring peace to restless spirits who have not moved on.

It is not enough, says Petry, to force ghosts to leave a place unless they are willing to move on to the afterlife. Simply forcing them to go away often means they will leave for only a little while or will take up residence somewhere else. Being able to communicate quietly with

ghosts, he can better explain to them why they would be better off moving on to the spirit world.

He says that the high-tech gear used by ghost hunters can be helpful, but more often just scares the spirits away temporarily: "Ghosts are like cats—they can disappear quite easily," Petry explains.

> Some [ghost hunting] teams go in with lasers, recorders, flashing cameras, ringing cell phones, humming motors. They disturb the area with excessive noise and light, and the phenomena take a powder [leave]. In one investigation I did with a group of tech people, I could literally see the ghosts disappear in front of us. When I visited the same area five hours later with no tech people, the ghosts reappeared.[64]

A Controversial Topic

No matter how confident psychics and ghost hunters are about the value of their work, they recognize that many people do not recognize the existence of ghosts. "It's kind of funny how the majority of people on this planet admit they believe in ghosts," says Grace Donne, "but the supposed authorities—the scientific world—denies their existence."[65]

Ghost hunter Joshua P. Warren agrees, saying that technology has already provided amazing clues that spirits do exist and sometimes haunt many places throughout the world. Although skeptics still question that evidence, Warren is confident that science will someday provide proof of the existence of ghosts. "The scientific method is still the best one we have when it comes to seeking truth," he says. "That's why we must use it in our quests to explore the unknown."[66]

Source Notes

Introduction: "I Guess No One Wanted to Live Here"

1. Martha, telephone interview, November 6, 2008.
2. Martha, telephone interview.
3. Martha, telephone interview.
4. Martha, telephone interview.
5. Martha, telephone interview.
6. Martha, telephone interview.
7. Martha, telephone interview.
8. Elle, personal interview, November 19, 2008, Minneapolis, Minnesota.

Chapter 1: Why Ghosts Haunt

9. Grace Donne, personal interview, June 14, 2007, Alexandria, Minnesota.
10. Quoted in News24.com, "Tsunami Ghosts Cause Terror," January 14, 2005. www.news24.com.
11. Quoted in Frederick Stonehouse, *Haunted Lakes II.* Duluth, MN: Lake Superior Port Cities, 2000, p. 35.
12. Troy Taylor, "The Greenbrier Ghost." www.prairieghosts.com.
13. Taylor, "The Greenbrier Ghost."
14. Quoted in Taylor, "The Greenbrier Ghost."
15. Katie Letcher Lyle, "The Greenbrier Ghost: The Only Ghost to Testify in a Murder Trial." www.wonderfulwv.com.

Chapter 2: Hauntings in the Great Outdoors

16. Brad Steiger, *Real Ghosts, Restless Spirits, and Haunted Places.* Canton, MI: Visible Ink, 2003, p. 496.
17. Quoted in Steiger, *Real Ghosts,* p. 496.
18. Quoted in Mark Moran and Mark Sceurman, eds., *Weird Hauntings: True Tales of Ghostly Places.* New York: Sterling, 2006, p. 140.
19. Quoted in Moran and Sceurman, *Weird Hauntings,* p. 140.
20. Quoted in Troy Taylor, *Weird Illinois: Your Travel Guide to Illinois' Local Legends and Best Kept Secrets.* New York: Sterling, 2005, p. 59.
21. Quoted in Taylor, *Weird Illinois,* p. 60.
22. Quoted in Taylor, *Weird Illinois,* p. 60.
23. Taylor, "Inez Clarke." www.prairieghosts.com.

24. Quoted in Taylor, "Inez Clarke."
25. Taylor, "Inez Clarke."
26. Paul White, personal interview, December 3, 2008, Minneapolis, Minnesota.
27. International Ghost Hunter Society. www.geocities.com.

Chapter 3: Ghosts on the Move

28. Valerie Robertson, "Maco Light: The Legend of Joe Baldwin," *North Brunswick Magazine Online.* www.thenbm.com.
29. Quoted in Robertson, "Maco Light."
30 Taylor, *Weird Illinois*, p. 53.
31. Taylor, *Weird Illinois*, p. 53.
32. Quoted in The Jeff Rense Program, "Prince Edward Says He and Film Crew Saw a Ghost Ship." www.rense.com.
33. Quoted in The Jeff Rense Program, "Prince Edward."
34. Quoted in The Jeff Rense Program, "Prince Edward."
35. Quoted in The Jeff Rense Program, "Prince Edward."
36. Quoted in The Jeff Rense Program, "Prince Edward."
37. Quoted in Moran and Sceurman, *Weird Hauntings*, p. 53.
38. Quoted in Moran and Sceurman, *Weird Hauntings*, p. 53.
39. Quoted in Moran and Sceurman, *Weird Hauntings*, pp. 53–54.
40. Quoted in Moran and Sceurman, *Weird Hauntings*, p. 54.
41. Quoted in Moran and Sceurman, *Weird Hauntings*, p. 54.

Chapter 4: Ghosts Inside

42. Janet Brennan, "Incarcerated Spooks of Scotland," *Fate*, June 2006, p. 22.
43. Benjamin Radford, "Courthouse 'Ghost' Video Mystery Solved," June 21, 2007. www.livescience.com.
44. Quoted in Steiger, *Real Ghosts*, p. 294.
45. Quoted in the Astral World, "Richard Harris's Ghost." www.theastralworld.com.
46. Quoted in The Astral World, "Richard Harris's Ghost."
47. Quoted in Bruce Morton, "Tips for Guests to the Lincoln Bedroom," CNN.com. www.cnn.com.
48. Quoted in Taylor, *Weird Illinois*, p. 193.
49. Quoted in Taylor, *Weird Illinois*, p. 193.

Chapter 5: Good-Bye to Haunting Spirits

50. Grace Donne, telephone interview.
51. Quoted in Katya Cengel, "Creeping Up on Ghosts," *Louisville* (KY) *Courier-Journal*.com, October 3, 2003. www.courier-journal.com.
52. Quoted in Cengel, "Creeping Up on Ghosts."
53. Gary Jensen, telephone interview, January 1, 2009.
54. Jensen, telephone interview.
55. Elle, personal interview.
56. Jensen, telephone interview.
57. Joshua P. Warren, "Basics of Detecting and 'Busting' Ghosts," *Fate*, April 2004, p. 41.

58. Quoted in Tom and Lisa Butler, "Electronic Voice Phenomena," *Fate*, March 2004, p. 26.
59. Quoted in Raymond Castile, "Who Ya Gonna Call? www.stateofhorror.com.
60. Quoted in Castile, "Who Ya Gonna Call?"
61. Quoted in Castile, "Who Ya Gonna Call?"
62. Jill, personal interview, June 28, 2007, Minneapolis, Minnesota.
63. Jill, personal interview.
64. Quoted in Rosemary Ellen Guiley, "He Sees the Dead," *Fate*, March 2007, pp. 51–52.
65. Grace Donne, telephone interview.
66. Warren, "Basics of Detecting and 'Busting' Ghosts."

For Further Research

Books

Jeff Belanger, *Who's Haunting the White House? The President's Mansion and the Ghosts Who Live There*. New York: Sterling, 2008.

Rosemary Ellen Guiley, *Ghosts and Haunted Places*. New York: Chelsea House, 2008.

Michael Norman, *Haunted Homeland*. New York: Forge, 2006.

Rebecca Stefoff, *Secrets of the Supernatural: Ghosts and Spirits*. New York: Marshall Cavendish, 2008.

Michael Teitelbaum, *Ghosts and Real-Life Ghost Hunters*. New York: Franklin Watts, 2008.

Web Sites

American Association-Electronic Voice Phenomena (www.aaevp.com). This is a very helpful Web site that includes the latest findings in EVP research and provides samples of some of the most interesting EVP transmissions.

American Society for Psychical Research (www.aspr.com). This organization investigates claims of ghosts and hauntings and also has a number of links on its Web site to information on a number paranormal events.

Committee for Skeptical Inquiry (www.csicop.com). This organization encourages critical investigation of ghosts and hauntings based on scientific principles. The site provides excellent links to articles by skeptics who point out what they see as weaknesses in many ghost hunting investigations.

Discovery Channel's Psychic and Paranormal Web Site (www.discovery channel.co.uk/paranormal/index. shtml). This is a very appealing site, with discussion of paranormal events throughout the world. It includes a well-maintained glossary of terms used by ghost hunters and a section on the world's most haunted places.

Ghost Research Society (www.ghost research.org). This group investigates ghosts, using the most high-tech instruments and tools. The site has links to some of the most famous haunting cases and how researchers used equipment in their investigations.

Ghostvillage.com (www.ghostvillage. com). A very interesting site that features an almost limitless range of personal narratives—real-life encounters with ghosts. The site also has links to interesting articles on the latest ghost research.

Index

About the Author

Gail B. Stewart is the author of more than 240 books for children and young adults. She received her bachelor's degree from Gustavus Adolphus College, and did her graduate work at the University of Minnesota and the University of St. Thomas. She and her husband, Carl, live in Minneapolis. They have three grown sons, two dogs, and a cat.

MW01103383

MAR - - 2010